BUG BOOKS

Ladybird

Karen Hartley and Chris Macro

Heinemann
LIBRARY

www.heinemann.co.uk/library
Visit our website to find out more information about Heinemann Library books.

To order:
 Phone 44 (0) 1865 888066
 Send a fax to 44 (0) 1865 314091
 Visit the Heinemann Bookshop at www.heinemann.co.uk/library to browse our catalogue and order online.

First published in Great Britain by Heinemann Library, Halley Court, Jordan Hill, Oxford OX2 8EJ, part of Harcourt Education.
Heinemann is a registered trademark of Harcourt Education Ltd.

Editorial: Clare Lewis and Katie Shepherd
Design: Ron Kamen, Michelle Lisseter and Bridge Creative Services Limited
Illustrations: Alan Fraser at Pennant Illustration
Picture Research: Maria Joannou
Production: Helen McCreath

Printed and bound in China by South China Printers

13 digit ISBN 978 0 431 01833 1 (hardback)
10 09 08 07 06
10 9 8 7 6 5 4 3 2 1

13 digit ISBN 978 0 431 01897 3 (paperback)
11 10 09 08 07
10 9 8 7 6 5 4 3 2 1

British Library Cataloguing in Publication Data
Hartley, Karen
Bug Books: Ladybird - 2nd Edition
595.7'69
A full catalogue record for this book is available from the British Library.

Acknowledgements
The publishers would like to thank the following for permission to reproduce photographs:
Alamy Images p.**26** (Elisabeth Coelfen); Bubbles p.**29** (Thurston); Bruce Coleman Ltd pp.**25** (D Austen), **5** (W Cheng Ward), **13** (J Grayson), **6**, **27** (P Kaya), **4**, **21** (H Reinhard), **19** (F Sauer), **12**, **28** (K Taylor); FLPA p.**15** (J Meul/ Foto Natura); NHPA pp.**8** (S Dalton), **20** (D Middleton); Oxford Scientific Films pp. **17** (P Franklin), **18** (A MacEwen), **10**, **11** (A Ramage), **22** (T Shepherd); Premaphotos pp.**9**, **16**, **23**, **24** (K Preston-Mafham); Science Photo Library p.**7** (J Burgess).

Cover photograph reproduced with permission of Corbis (Ralph A Clevenger).

The publishers would like to thank Nancy Harris for her assistance in the preparation of this book.

Every effort has been made to contact copyright holders of any material reproduced in this book. Any omissions will be rectified in subsequent printings if notice is given to the publishers.

Any words appearing in the text in bold, **like this**, are explained in the Glossary

Contents

What are ladybirds?

Ladybirds are **insects**. They have six legs and two pairs of wings. They have a round body like half a ball.

A ladybird is a small **beetle**.
Most ladybirds are red or yellow
with black spots. Some are black
or brown with white spots.

There are many types of ladybird in the world. We are going to look at red ladybirds with black spots.

feelers

eyes

jaws

Ladybirds have two eyes for seeing up, down, backwards, and forwards. Ladybirds have two **feelers** for touching. They have jaws for biting.

Eyed ladybird

Ladybirds are different sizes.
An eyed ladybird is about as
long as your fingernail.

pin

The 16-spot ladybird is much smaller.
It is only as big as the top of a pin!

How are ladybirds born?

In spring and summer it is warm. Female ladybirds lay eggs on the undersides of leaves. The eggs are **oval** and pale yellow.

larva

After four days a baby
hatches from each egg.
It is called a **larva** or grub.

When the **larvae** hatch they grow very quickly. They lose their skins and grow new ones. The larvae turn dark blue with yellow or red spots.

After four weeks each larva starts to change. It is now called a **pupa**. A week later it splits open and out crawls a ladybird.

new wings

What do ladybirds eat?

Some ladybirds eat the leaves of plants. Most ladybirds eat tiny green insects called aphids.

aphids

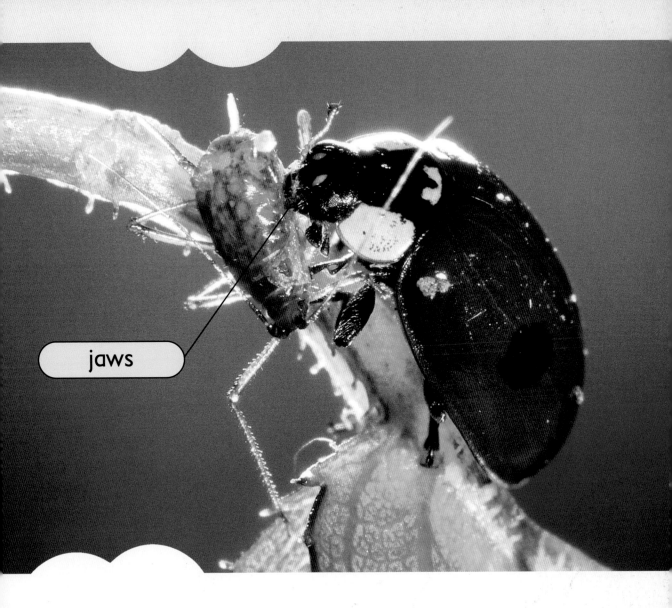

jaws

Ladybirds eat lots of aphids. They catch them in their strong jaws.

ant

Ants eat aphids too. Sometimes they attack ladybirds. They want to stop the ladybirds from eating the aphids.

Not many animals eat ladybirds. Their bright colours warn **enemies** that they do not taste nice. Some spiders eat ladybirds.

How do ladybirds move?

Ladybirds use their wings to fly.
They fly to look for food. When they
land they fold their wings away.

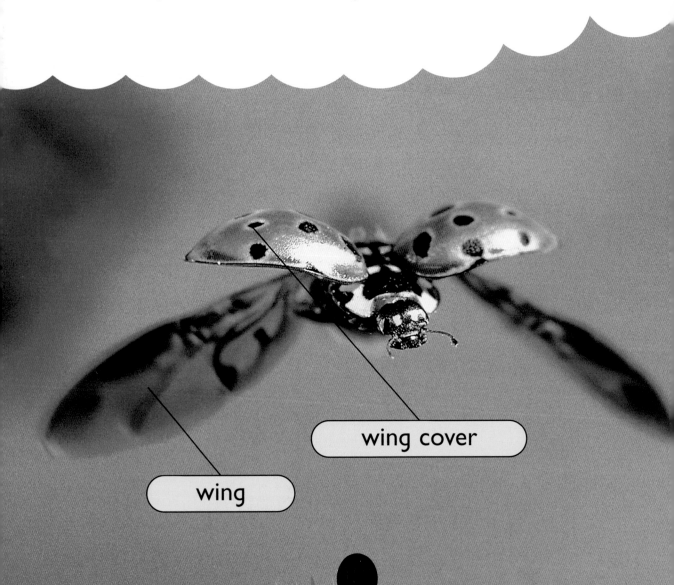

wing cover

wing

A ladybird can crawl very quickly.

It uses its six feet to hold on.

Where do ladybirds live?

Ladybirds live where they can find food.
They eat aphids that live on the leaves
and stems of flowers.

You will find ladybirds where there are lots of flowers and trees. Most gardens have ladybirds living in them.

How long do ladybirds live?

Most ladybirds live through
the spring, summer and autumn.
Many die in the winter.

Ladybirds do not like cold weather.
In the winter they **huddle** together for
warmth. You can sometimes see them
under a big stone or on a tree trunk.

Why do people like ladybirds?

Ladybirds eat garden pests that harm plants and flowers. People who have gardens like ladybirds because they help their plants.

Sometimes farmers bring ladybirds to their farms and **orchards**. The ladybirds eat aphids and other insects that kill the farmers' plants.

People like ladybirds because they are cute. Sometimes people make toys that look like ladybirds.

Ladybirds are special. They do not have ears, so they cannot hear. They feel **vibrations** with their feet. This helps them know if something is coming.

Thinking about ladybirds

Do you remember what happens to a
ladybird's eggs after she lays them?
How do ladybirds grow?

Bug map

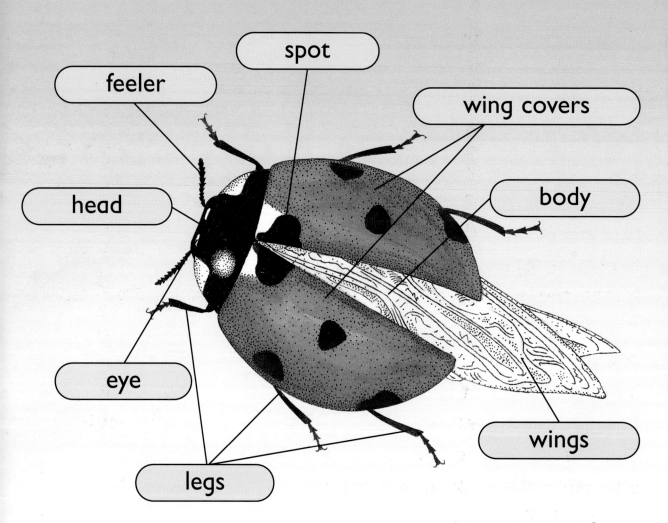

spot

feeler

wing covers

head

body

eye

legs

wings

Actual size

Glossary

beetle an insect that has hard wing covers to protect its wings

enemies other animals that might attack or eat a ladybird

feelers two long thin tubes that stick out from the head of an insect. They are used to smell, feel, or hear.

hatch to be born out of an egg

huddle to crowd together with others

insect a small creature with six legs

larva the grub that hatches from an insect egg. More than one are called larvae.

orchard a place where fruit trees are grown

oval a shape that is almost round, like a squashed circle

pupa the step between larva and adult, when an insect is enclosed in a cocoon

vibration the shaking that happens in the air or on the ground when an animal moves

Index

More books to read

Creepy Creatures: Ladybirds, Monica Hughes (Heinemann Library 2005)